REFRAME
your thinking
around
AUTISM

HOLLY BRIDGES

FOREWORD BY STEPHEN W. PORGES

REFRAME
your thinking
around
AUTISM

How the Polyvagal Theory and Brain Plasticity
Help Us Make Sense of Autism

Jessica Kingsley *Publishers*
London and Philadelphia

Quote on page 13 is reproduced from Collins 2004 with
kind permission from Tessler Literary Agency.
Quote on page 18 is reproduced from Feldenkrais 1981 with
kind permission from Meta Publications.
Quote on page 52 is reproduced from *How the Brain Represents*
the Body: Insights from Neurophysiology and Psychology with
kind permission from Michael Graziano.
Quote on page 47 is reproduced from Dispenza 2013 with kind permission from Hay House.

First published in 2015
by Jessica Kingsley Publishers
73 Collier Street
London N1 9BE, UK
and
400 Market Street, Suite 400
Philadelphia, PA 19106, USA

www.jkp.com

Library of Congress Cataloging in Publication Data
Bridges, Holly.
Reframe your thinking around autism: how the polyvagal
theory and brain plasticity help us make
sense of autism / Holly Bridges.
pages cm
Includes bibliographical references and index.
ISBN 978-1-84905-672-4 (alk. paper)
1. Autism in children--Treatment. 2. Affect (Psychology) 3. Social interaction. I. Title.
RJ506.A9B745 2015
618.92'85882--dc23
2015008375

British Library Cataloguing in Publication Data
A CIP catalogue record for this book is available from the British Library

ISBN 978 1 84905 672 4
eISBN 978 1 78450 177 8

Printed and bound in the United States

MIX
Paper from
responsible sources
FSC® C013483

Contents

Disclaimer

The author and publisher disclaim any warranties (express or implied), merchantability, or fitness for any particular purpose. The author and publisher shall in no event be held liable to any party for any direct, indirect, punitive, special, incidental or other consequential damages arising directly or indirectly from any use of this material, which is provided 'as is', and without warranties.

As always, the advice of a competent legal, medical, or other health professional should be sought. The author and publisher do not warrant the performance, effectiveness or applicability of any sites listed or linked to in this book. All links are for information purposes only and are not warranted for content, accuracy or any other implied or explicit purpose.

The author takes full responsibility for representing and interpreting the ideas related to the Polyvagal Theory. The author's interpretations and representations of the Polyvagal Theory may vary in intent and accuracy from the writings and presentations by Dr Stephen W. Porges.

The author takes full responsibility for representing and interpreting the ideas related to the Nine Essentials of the Anat Baniel Method. The author's interpretations and representations of the Nine Essentials of the Anat Baniel Method may vary in intent and accuracy from the writings and presentations by Anat Baniel.

Foreword

by Stephen W. Porges

In the academic research community, autism is discussed as a brain disorder with a genetic basis. Yet no specific biomarker can diagnose autism. While the research community is focused on identifying specific mechanisms underlying autism, families are searching for an understanding of the disorder that will enable them to manage their child and to develop a strategy to optimize their child's potential. In response to this disparate agenda, Holly Bridges has written *Reframe Your Thinking Around Autism*.

This is a succinctly written book with engaging graphics that provides a new optimistic approach to conceptualize autism. Rather than focusing on the clinical diagnostic tools that have been used to define autism, Holly Bridges focuses on linking many of the compromised functions that are experienced by autistics to features of the Polyvagal Theory, a theory I developed. She accurately notes that the features of the social engagement system described in the theory are depressed in autistics. A depressed social engagement system results in poor facial affect, auditory hypersensitivities, lack of prosody in voice, and an autonomic state that under challenge will shift to support Fight/Flight behaviours or shutdown. This disruption in autonomic state would interfere both with ingestive and digestive processes, symptoms frequently observed in autism. Using the Polyvagal Theory as an organizing principle she introduces a variety of intervention models that potentially could function as neural exercises (i.e. brain plasticity) to rehabilitate the social engagement system and to optimize autonomic regulation.

Unlike most books on autism that are targeted to professionals who evaluate and treat, this unique and readable book effectively connects to the families and the people who directly interact with individuals with autism.

Stephen W. Porges, PhD, Professor of Psychiatry, University of North Carolina, and author of *The Polyvagal Theory: Neurophysiological Foundations of Emotions, Attachment, Communication, and Self-regulation*

Preface

Reframe Your Thinking Around Autism is a smart, easy-to-grasp book that offers a whole new paradigm for understanding and working with autism.

It explains in simple language the work of American neuroscientist Dr Stephen Porges, and his Polyvagal Theory. The Polyvagal Theory suggests that autism may not be a neurological disorder, but a learnt response of the body to early stressors. It supplies not only a plausible answer to the question 'What is autism?', but it also explains *why* there is a spectrum. This theory is beautiful and allows for the possibility of real change.

So many people do change on the autism spectrum. Some people are non-verbal, only to find that they later find their voice. Others can become much more proficient and comfortable in company as they mature. Some parents have described their child as neurotypical only to find after some event that they were not, and some document that the symptoms of autism in their child have been completely reversed.

The Polyvagal Theory makes sense of this change. It allows us to see past the diagnosis of autism and opens new doors to therapy and healing.

1. Where We Are

> Think of it: a disability is usually defined in terms of what is missing…but autism…is as much about what is abundant as what is missing, an over-expression of the very traits that make our species unique.
>
> *Paul Collins (2004)*

Autism is a part of a life. The people who experience it have a life, and autism is a part of it. A lot of people with autism find that it gives them heightened intuition; they feel it can inform their life beautifully, as much as it can be a disruption. Autists don't necessarily want to become normal, but they do want to engage with the world better.

Autists are bright people stuck in a body that doesn't respond for them. They are shut off by their body from the rest of the world. This can be frightening and difficult, and it does not always bring out their best. Autism can be mild or it can be full-blown. Autists can have an openness to the world that sometimes shuts down, or they can be always shut down. For the autist it feels as if they are shut out.

People with autism are less able than other people to interact with the world. The *Diagnostic and Statistical Manual of Mental Disorders, DSM-5* (American Psychological Association 2013) describes them as typically having deficits in two key areas:

- Persistent deficits in social communication and social interaction across multiple contexts:

  - Deficits in social-emotional reciprocity

- Deficits in nonverbal communicative behaviors used for social interaction

- Deficits in developing, maintaining, and understanding relationships.

- Restricted, repetitive patterns of behavior, interests, or activities:

  - Stereotyped or repetitive motor movements, use of objects, or speech

  - Insistence on sameness, inflexible adherence to routines, or ritualized patterns or verbal nonverbal behaviour

  - Highly restricted, fixated interests that are abnormal in intensity or focus

  - Hyper- or hyporeactivity to sensory input or unusual interests in sensory aspects of the environment.

Some people who study autism like to look in the brain for answers. But they haven't found any. Other people like to look to genetics for the reasons why people have it. But they haven't found any. Autism has everyone stumped.

2. What We Know

The exact cause is unknown. Although research suggests the likelihood of a genetic basis, there is no known genetic etiology and brain imaging techniques have not identified a clear common pathology. There is no single treatment and the effectiveness of particular interventions is supported by only limited data.

James C. McPartland and Ami Klin

Science likes to look at the brain, and it likes to be rational. We have grown up with science and the thinking that the brain is in charge, that we are rational human beings with rational brains. We like to think we are clever. We like to think we are much cleverer than the beasts.

It is nice to be clever and rational, but isn't there something missing in the picture?

Now, animals are smart. They think, they nurture, they love, they interact, and they can communicate across vast distances (like elephants and dolphins). They, like us, have a wonderful nervous system that allows them to see and hear and adapt and interact. Animals have a huge intelligence, as animals. You try being hunted by a lion and see who's clever!

Like lions and tigers and iguanas and dolphins and elephants, we humans also have a nervous system. We need our nervous system to survive. Our nervous system helps us to see and hear; it helps us to move, to run and to fight. Our nervous system informs our brain; it takes in information and tells us what's going on and it attunes us to our world. It is our *other* intelligence and we share it with all other animals. We humans are lucky; we can do all that animals can, and we can speak, drive a car and fire a gun.

So our human brains are more complex; we are clever. We humans like to be clever, we like to be the *most* clever – *better than all the animals* – and so we have put a lot of emphasis on the importance of our brains. This is good, as our brains *are* very special: they can create, they can think up all sorts of wonderful things. But are they everything? When it comes to understanding people, most people think so.

So our brains are the best and we have become very good at being in charge of them. We have become very good at 'mind over matter'. We have learnt to be in control of ourselves, to use the power of the mind, and this is what we teach.

Our approach to autism is the same. We look at it as a brain problem, then we manage behaviour, we train behaviour, we train mindfulness…but we all know this doesn't quite work. There is something missing.

Now, autists are generally really smart. They might not be able to communicate this to you – their tongue may get tied, or they may not be able to speak much at all – but they are still in there, thinking, creating and designing with their wonderful brains. So if it's not the brain…

3. Something New – The Polyvagal Theory

Very often there are better ways of thinking which open up new vistas and make the unthinkable real and put the impossible within our grasp.

Moshe Feldenkrais

The Polyvagal Theory was proposed and developed by the neuroscientist Dr Stephen Porges. Dr Porges studies the way that the body and brain interact and his Polyvagal Theory is a theory about our developing nervous system and how it affects who we are. 'Poly' means many and 'vagus' refers to our vagus nerve.

The vagus nerve is a cranial nerve that conveys sensory information about the state of the body's organs to the central nervous system. It innervates the organs and it communicates the state of the body to the brain. In Latin, *vagus* means 'wandering', and this nerve wanders all over the body, keeping information flowing. There are two parts: an older one and a newer one.

The Polyvagal Theory, in a nutshell, is this. The body has two systems. One runs up and down with the body and brain continuously chatting, communicating about how things are going. When things are running smoothly it is bi-directional – energy goes up and down from toes to head, and back again. There is flow and communication. The other system goes round and round. It rolls through the various organs in your abdomen, making energy and keeping things clean and healthy.

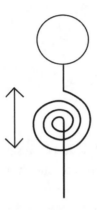

These two systems work side by side, simultaneously. They talk to each other day and night, relaying information and keeping things operating…unless there is a problem.

When there is a problem, something threatening like a lion attack, the systems' flow changes. Suddenly the up and down flow doesn't happen so well, and the round and round cycle seizes up. All the energy that was previously making you feel well and happy is suddenly being used to put you into red alert.

The energy that once flowed so tranquilly up and down is now being thrust up towards your brain to make you concentrate on the lion. The direction is now all one way. You are in survival mode, you are ready for action. This is the primary survival mechanism, Fight or Flight. The body is primed for action.

Now, ordinarily, once the lion walks away, once the threat passes, this mechanism relaxes and things go back to normal. There is once again room for thinking about other things like smiling and chatting and engaging with the world.

But what if the lion doesn't walk away? What if he gets closer...and closer...? When this happens, we have another option – to freeze. Like a rabbit caught in the headlights, we can also stop absolutely stock still. When the lion gets too close, we can faint, or go into partial paralysis, or a dead stop. This is called 'Immobilization'. It is a primary defence: when there is no other option, we play dead.

It really should be called FFI, not just Fight or Flight, because we have three survival mechanisms: Fight or Flight or Immobilization – depending on the level of adversity we are facing. Immobilization is an adaptive function; we use it next, when Fight or Flight is not an option. Porges says that science has mostly forgotten about this function, but that it is vital to understanding not just autism, but depression and all sorts of other human difficulties.

The FFI response is an important part of our safety and security and it can come in very handy. However, it is not so handy if it turns itself on all the time without there being much to worry about, and this is exactly what Dr Stephen Porges thinks happens with autism. He thinks that the FFI system in the autist is a bit, or a lot, twitchy.

Porges' ideas examine the notion of safety. When our safety is assured, we are calm and engaged with our world. When our safety is in question, our brain and body talk to each other quite differently. When we are calm we can be open; when we are Immobilized, we are shut off. As a body experience, we are shut down.

The Polyvagal Theory is a massive paradigm shift in understanding behaviour because it stresses the importance of the physiological state – the body – in understanding the mind. The theory is bi-directional; it is not mind over matter. Rather than one being in charge of the other, the brain and the body talk to each other continuously. They talk, they work in tandem. It is a bipartisan relationship.

4. The Polyvagal Theory in More Detail

> Autists have an inability to regulate their visceral state in the presence of others. Basically, the child's vagal nervous system is not sufficiently developed to regulate in a complex setting.
>
> *Dr Stephen Porges*

Our bodies have an autonomic nervous system. This system works mostly without our control. We breathe, our hearts pump, we digest food and make blood cells all without much conscious attention. Our bodies take care of us and as long as we put in the right food and water and exercise we are mostly okay. Our bodies work pretty efficiently without our having to think about it; it's mostly automatic.

There are two parts to our nervous system: the parasympathetic and the sympathetic-adrenal. When your parasympathetic system is in action you are open and calm. Your digestive system rolls comfortably, your heart rate is down, you have control of your bladder, your breathing is normal, your mouth has saliva, you can swallow easily and your eyes are engaged with the world. The parasympathetic system allows a calm state for good health, nourishment, species reproduction and restoration of cells.

When you are in Fight or Flight, the sympathetic-adrenal system is on duty. In this state your heart rate is accelerated, your breathing is shallow, your saliva dries up and it is hard to swallow; you can lose control over your bowel and bladder; ingestion and digestion are difficult; your eyes dilate; adrenaline is secreted. Now your focus is on your body's safety.

When you are in Immobilization mode, you are no longer operating from the sympathetic-adrenal, but you have passed the fast action into the still mode regulated by an ancient branch of the vagus that is used by animals like reptiles to defend by appearing to be inanimate. Your body slows, your heart rate slows, your breathing slows, your blood pressure drops, but your digestion, bladder and bowel control, eyes and ears are offline – there is nobody home.

The vagus nerve

The vagus nerve is the communication highway, carrying information and connecting the nervous system to the brain and to all the major organs of the body, especially the gut. The vagus nerve works as a bi-directional conduit, relaying information about how you are feeling up and down the body. It allows the body to communicate with the brain, and it is regulated by the autonomic nervous system, which is in charge of the FFI.

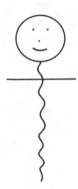

The vagus nerve is part of the parasympathetic nervous system and can influence the sympathetic-adrenal system. It is a powerful regulator of visceral (inner body) feelings and tactile pain thresholds. It regulates the gut and the heart; it can raise or reduce cortisol secretion. It can act to soothe the body, it can mobilize the body into action, or it can shut it down. The vagus nerve will read what you need and respond.

> The vagus nerve directly supports the behaviours needed to engage and disengage with the environment.
>
> *Dr Stephen Porges*

The vagus nerve is our 'action station'. If it is left on too long, it can lead to ingestive and digestive problems, general discomfort and restlessness, sleep disruption and visceral (internal) pain. If your vagal system is on high alert for such a long time, your body can get to feel quite sore and everything can feel quite out of kilter.

These on-too-long vagal symptoms may describe the many physical difficulties associated with autism. Autists often have digestive problems, restlessness, sleep disruption and visceral pain – we just have never understood why.

5. The Social Engagement System

As humans we balance the need for social interactions with the need for safety. The need for safety is paramount. Immobilization is an adaptive function.

Dr Stephen Porges

There are two parts to the vagus nerve: the old and the new. The old vagus regulates the organs in the body below the diaphragm, especially the gut, and it connects to the heart. When things are running smoothly the old vagus conducts the overall flow of the digestive system and organs of the body. It is also involved in the release of hormones to help you with your day: dopamine (calm), serotonin (happy) and cortisol (stress).

When things are not going well and the system is under duress, the smooth flow of the old vagus is suppressed. The digestive system is shut down or slowed, there is a disconnection from the heart – from feeling – and there can be reflexive defecation. This physiological response is shared with other animals in response to threat: they, we, freeze. It is a safety mechanism. The old vagus enables this defensive response.

The new vagus is regulated by the parasympathetic nervous system which operates when we are calm and safe. In this state we are open and engaged with our world, and we spend our time growing, healing and restoring the body. The vagus nerve, when we are in this calm state, works closely with the social engagement system. The vagus nerve gets its information about what to do next through the social engagement system.

The social engagement system involves neural pathways embedded in several cranial nerves that develop *in utero*. It essentially controls the muscles we need to engage with our world. It controls the eye muscles – seeing, looking, engaging; the facial muscles – facial affect; the middle ear muscles – smiling, laughing, chewing, ingesting; the laryngeal and pharyngeal muscles – voice prosody; and the head-turning muscles – social gesture and orientation.

The vagus nerve chats to the social engagement system – it relays information to and from it. Information comes in via the eyes, ears and mouth and travels through to the body via the vagus nerve. Depending on whether the information coming in is 'safe', the vagus nerve will instruct the body to parasympathetic behaviour (calm, engaged, smiling, open) or sympathetic (argue, move away, shut down).

These two systems are in direct communication; they support each other. They work to allow the person to make sense of the world, to interact, to be safe. When we are safe, we use the social engagement system to communicate verbally and non-verbally. We smile, we observe faces, we listen, we talk, we incline our heads and we raise our eyebrows. We do these things because we want to, we do them because our bodies can do them, and we do them when our bodies are set to the parasympathetic.

> These 'social' muscles function as filters that limit and allow social stimuli. Hence they determine the individual's engagement with the social environment.
>
> *Dr Stephen Porges*

Our social engagement system allows us to use our eyes and ears and face to connect with the world, to communicate.

It is unique to mammals. Iguanas, lizards and snakes do not have the necessary system to make eye contact, to smile and communicate with their friends. Mammals do. Lions hang out together. Monkeys chat and share food. Cats, horses, giraffes and rabbits all groom one another and spend time together. We are like them, yet we have an even more complex brain and an even more complex social network.

The social engagement system is how we engage with the world. We smile, we speak, we look, we listen, we laugh, we turn our heads; we breathe easily and let the world in. The world comes in and we come out, through the social engagement system.

The social engagement system operates when we feel safe. It enables friendly, social interaction and this helps us to be in a calm state for good health and restoration of cells. However, the social engagement system does not work so well when we are in Fight, Flight or Immobilization. It more or less goes offline as we are engaged in looking after our safety.

You don't need social niceties when you are running or fighting for your life, and you don't need them when you are frozen to the ground in fright. The brain diverts attention to where it is needed, and social engagement has less priority when your brain perceives you are in danger. As with your digestive system, in times of danger the social engagement system is automatically turned down or off.

Like lions and monkeys, we save our grooming and hanging out with friends for when we are in a parasympathetic (calm) state. When lions are angry or scared, they are less likely to be open to making friends and having fun as they need to be focused on staying alive. When their sympathetic system is activated, there is not much need for the social system to be operating either. Their energy is needed for safety.

Generally our old system and our new system are in perfect harmony. We are calm, we interact, our heart rate is normal, we can digest food easily, and we breathe calmly. As well, we can speak easily, make good eye contact, smile, turn our heads gently, and listen to the nuances in a conversation. We can move and interact with grace as well as digest food and repair our cells. When we are calm there is enough energy to go around.

As we grow we learn to use our body to modulate our environment. As well as learning to interact when things are good, we can also learn to do other things when things aren't as harmonious. We can learn to use our ears to block out noise that is too loud, we can learn to make good eye contact and smile at new people to make them feel safe, and we can learn to breathe slowly to calm ourselves down. We learn to do these things with our body. We learn to use our eyes, our ears, our mouths and voices to modulate our environment. It gives us a good level of control over what's going on around us.

If we somehow don't have a level of control over what is going on around us we can get a bit stressed. Our cortisol will go up. Depending on the level of adversity, we might go into Fight or Flight. We might go into anger or aggression, or we may withdraw and move away until we feel better. When we get back to being calm we can get back to interacting nicely with people again. If we are Immobilized we might faint, or disassociate, and then it can take quite a bit longer to get back to feeling like ourselves, back to a calm operating system.

The social engagement system is our new evolutionary software. When you are small you learn to operate it.

You learn how to smile appropriately, you learn what noises to listen for, you learn to look for comfort and you can learn to use it to calm down. You learn to 'read' what is going on in your external world and how to respond to it. You learn to integrate your brain and your body to best respond to your external world.

But what if this does not happen so well? What if when you were young you didn't learn to use this social software? What if when you were very small, your system had been distressed for some reason and all your energy had been diverted to your safety? What if you had gone into the Fight, Flight or Immobilization response and, being so young, you had not known how to get yourself back out? What if your FFI had just been left on too long?

This is the Polyvagal Theory. Dr Porges thinks that many autists are people for whom, as infants, the vagal system was diverted to the body's safety and this then became the focus for the growing child. The body system, Immobilized, becomes painful or agitated, digestion is difficult and the child's focus turns inward. Interaction with the outside world is compromised.

As the child's focus turns inward and less focused on the outside world, the natural integration of the social engagement system does not take place with as much ease. As the sympathetic system does not allow easy access to the social engagement system, the child does not learn how to use their system well. They do not learn to control their social software, to drive it, and so it ends up working more on autopilot and their FFI is like a runaway train.

Social situations, because they are highly complex, require a well-functioning social engagement system; otherwise they become a minefield of sensations. Autists, because they have not set up the software needed to process the information properly, can read threat in the environment and go quite quickly through FFI, to shut down.

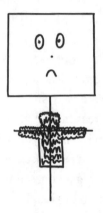

Autism is like being given an itchy jumper to wear by your Granny. While all the other kids in the playground are off running and jumping in the playground, the autist is stuck dealing with Granny's itchy jumper

All sorts of noises, smells and sights come in and the autist has not learnt how to regulate the information, nor how to regulate the body's response. Their system overloads, it triggers the FFI and they Immobilize.

The theory is that autists have a reduced capacity to engage with the world because they have not learnt to process complex social data; this triggers the FFI and it goes off willy-nilly.

This can be slight or profound. Some autists can learn some social skills but not be able to access them all the time; while for some, they virtually stay Immobilized.

Dr Porges thinks that autism is perhaps not a genetically determined neurological deficit, but a response to stress or trauma that happens quite early on for the child. He thinks that, for whatever reason, the vagus is disposed towards Immobilization, and because of this the child's nervous system does not get fully developed. It can be slight. It can be strong emotional trauma, a fear that presents *in utero* or at birth, a physical disruption of the vagal nerve, fever, antibiotics, vaccines, or a response to x, y, z.

The point is not *what* it is a result of, but *that* it is a fact that the child's system has been in a state of distress. Instead of the old and the new getting wired up together as they should, they end up sitting separately from each other. Instead of knitting together nicely from birth, the new system is there and the old system is there, but they haven't got to talking too well. So the baby misses out on the full integration of all that the social engagement system has to offer and the eyes, ears, face are all more, or less, offline.

This is where the 'autism spectrum', the 'continuum', comes in. The connection between the social engagement system and the vagus nerve is just that, a connection. It can be strong, it can be faulty, and it can be switched off under duress. It can be a bit strong, weak sometimes, high-functioning at other times.

We can all be a bit autistic, because it is a part of normal human function. We can all shut down in certain circumstances. Autists just do it frequently. Autism is a physical reality and it is part of our natural human experience.

> It can make a huge difference to the autist to understand that what is happening is a physiological response, that it is not 'them'... Informing the autist that this is just 'triggered circuitry' can be profoundly liberating for an autist.
>
> *Dr Stephen Porges*

The social engagement system literally links the face to the heart. Reptiles do not have this physical link. Not only do they not smile, but they cannot pay attention to their feelings. They are shut off from the heart – physically.

We, like other mammals, are not shut off from our heart. We have anatomy that allows us to feel, and to express what we feel. When the body is registering extreme stress, or fear, this mechanism switches off. When we are really angry or scared, it is much harder to feel the softness of the heart, we close off to it. We literally close our bodies off. Autists, more or less, have less ability to access their heart, and they can switch off from it faster than we can. They physically have a weaker link to their feelings, and being able to express their feelings.

> The neural control of the heart is neuroanatomically linked to the neural control of the muscles of the face and head.
>
> *Dr Stephen Porges*

The social engagement system
links the face to the heart.
It is how we show the world who we are.
If it has turned itself off, for whatever reason,
people cannot see what we are feeling.
We just look blank.
If we are constantly Immobilized,
we might even feel blank.

6. Living is an Embodied Experience

> Our body functions like a polygraph. We are continuously responding to people and places…we do this normally. If we do not feel safe, our polygraph is on high, we are in a chronic state of evaluation and defensiveness.
>
> *Dr Stephen Porges*

Dr Porges suggests that humans require constant interaction with others in order to develop and optimize their potential. Smiles, eye contact and laughter are all social and safety cues that work to make us feel safe with the people we are around. This is as much a physical process as an emotional one. Physically when we receive a cue, a smile, a frown, our bodies respond. If we feel secure our cortisol (stress hormone) may go down, our dopamine (calm hormone) may go up, we may breathe more slowly. If we feel unsafe, the opposite may occur.

These social cues elicit a biochemical response in our bodies that gets our bodies moving in a certain direction. This is all very subtle so we don't really notice it happening. It is subliminal, not something we consciously notice, but our bodies are constantly responding to each other. They are picking up messages and communicating all the time.

Living is an embodied experience. We experience the world through our bodies just as much as our minds. We are continually transmitting cues to each other's nervous system, and we are continuously assessing our environment, our world, for safety. Dr Porges suggests that we are like human polygraph machines; we evaluate the social environment and make the necessary behavioural adjustments. Often, we can relax and settle in to the occasion as we have learnt how.

The difference with autists is that their polygraphs are switched on high most of the time. They are generally in a constant scanning mode – checking for safety – but have not learnt to read the environment well. Autists have not learnt to read social cues appropriately and have not learnt to give out social cues. They do not easily smile or make appropriate facial gestures to calm people down.

It is normal for most people to operate with these cues. We need cues to understand our world, and we have receptors in our bodies that read and respond to these cues. Dr Porges calls these cues 'feature detectors'. Our vagal system – 80 per cent of which is sensory – is designed to respond to these cues and we unconsciously expect them from one another. We feel safe in an environment that gives out the appropriate cues and we like people who give us cues that make us feel good. Physically our sympathetic nervous system is soothed by safe cues from people.

At a subliminal, physical level our need for these positive cues has to be met. We know who we are and we feel safe when we feel well met. When we do not receive them we can feel unsafe. When people don't give us these cues we can feel betrayed, insulted, threatened, unloved and uncared for, because we need them in order to feel secure – at a subliminal level. We can feel disengaged and emotionally disconnected from the person without them, and we can go into our own heightened state of FFI.

Dr Porges suggests that as it is a subliminal activity, we can be unaware that this is what is happening or why we are feeling this way. He says that, as a society generally, we want to blame the person who is not emitting well – we view them as cold; we find it hard to trust them; we see them as mean, uncaring or stupid. The interpretation of the person's motivation is often negative. They are not to be trusted, something feels 'wrong'. If people were nice, they would smile, or laugh or look you in the eye.

Often we do not think further than this, we just listen to our automatic assessment. The trouble with autists is that they don't emit well, because they *can't*. Often they have gone into Immobilization, into shutdown mode, which is for them a very normal response. They may be feeling hungry, distressed, or anxious – not at all mean or uncaring, just switched off.

This can account for some of the bullying of autists in schools and other places. Having these cues met is a physical need, and when this is missing it is hard to feel comfortable. This is especially true for children (or adults) who might, for their own reasons, have their polygraph on high, and are also sensitive to their environment. The bullying of autists that occurs may be a way of others coping with the withdrawal of these cues. People rely on positive cues to feel safe.

Teaching ourselves and others to be aware of this can make a huge difference to how we respond to autists and can help us to take care of ourselves when we are feeling replete. It can also make a huge difference to the autist to understand that this is how others feel.

Be kind to yourself.
Make sure you make time for you.
Remember you have a sympathetic system too!
Take time out for a walk, or to ring a friend.
Ask someone over for a hug.
Be mindful that your needs matter
and that your autist can't necessarily meet them.
Taking care of yourself
engages your parasympathetic system,
and gives you grace.

7. Learning to Be

Trauma, or triggers of earlier trauma, brings profound and unexpected immobilization. When in trauma, we revert to 'older' circuitry – we faint, we immobilize, or disassociate.

Dr Stephen Porges

Usually we learn to integrate our social engagement system very slowly and subtly as babies and this learning takes place almost unconsciously. Babies slowly learn to use their body. They learn to drive their body like we learn to drive a car. You start off slowly, with fierce concentration on the most minute detail until you have mastered it, then you move on to the next thing and the next until all of a sudden you can use your feet on the pedals while steering, while looking out of the window and working out where you are going. But you have to start slowly: it takes a while before your mind can manage all that and drive at 100km an hour!

Autists haven't learnt how to use their body so well. For them, going out in public is like driving at 100km an hour without a licence. It is too fast, they can't process it. It is information overload, as their brains are not wired up for the experience.

Like learning to drive a car, babies spend their time wiring up their brain and their body. It is what they do. They will stare at their fingers for hours. They will look at their feet, their toes, your eyes. They will smile and get a response. They will bend and flex, bringing feet to head. Slowly but surely they are learning to be in their body, and learning how to use it to engage with the world. They have to learn that this leg, this foot, belongs to them, how to make eye good contact, to smile on cue; they have to learn how to think, and how to be. It is not all completely automatic.

Babies are pretty smart because their brains and autonomic nervous system are generally working nicely when they are born. They know they are in there, but they do need a lot of time to work out that they have a body and how to use it.

It is all rather haphazard at first, but it slowly comes together. Slowly they begin to direct their arms and legs; slowly they begin to delight in making their brain and body talk to each other, so they can move, so they can communicate, so they can be in the world.

Babies gently embark on the extraordinary journey of self-awareness. Their job for the first few years is to get the body and brain talking. They are learning to feel and also to make sense of feeling; they are creating awareness. Babies begin to construct a world of images in their minds and begin relating them to positive and negative feelings, moving, associating and belonging. Awareness starts off simply, in the body. Gradually it becomes an increasingly complex association between the body and the mind.

But what happens if it starts off a bit complex? What happens if, for whatever reason, the baby is in prolonged FFI? What happens if at some point the baby has become Immobilized? Being a baby, they have little or no way of making sense of this. They do not know *who* they are; they just know *that* they are. In many ways, who babies think they are *is* their body.

So, having experienced it, babies can associate themselves with Immobilization; it becomes part of what they are, what they do. They have not learnt to separate and control this response, as it happens very early and so becomes integrated with their sense of self. Immobilization becomes a default position and certain triggers will make the child revert back to it easily.

This default becomes a *learnt response*, and an *identity*, and both get reinforced over time. It becomes part of the child, part of who they think they are. The mechanism to their sympathetic-adrenal response is strong; they associate with fear and shut down as a normal response and they associate with being inwardly focused. It is not a matter of choice or control. It just happens and it slowly becomes a hardwired, physical response.

8. The Gifts of the Autist

Autists often are most gifted; they can become people who add enormous value to our evolving culture and our community. To name a few: Emily Dickinson, Charles Darwin, Michelangelo, Mozart, Einstein and Newton were all reported to have autistic traits of social and tactile sensitivities, obsessive routines, or awkward facial movements.

Autists also know that they are more than their body. As it is often so uncomfortable and unwieldy, autists tend to grow up feeling separate from their body. They sort of 'see' themselves in it and see themselves as being more than what they feel and do. They can see their body shutting down on them and they notice that they cannot interact as others do; that they have less choice and less access to fun and pleasure. Often it is not fun, but autists do gain a great deal of awareness by being imprisoned in this way.

An autist may become gifted because certain areas of their brain get to expand exponentially while they are compensating for their troubles. They might be socially awkward, but autists are often highly intuitive. Some, like Temple Grandin, can understand and empathize with animals at a level that the average neurotypical cannot and autists in general have a sensitivity that affords a higher level of awareness.

Autists do seem to gain a greater level of awareness than most. Often they can see things that others can't, and being able to see yourself as separate from your feelings is a thing to be desired. This is actually a trait that is envied by all aspiring Buddhists! Buddhists feel they become more enlightened when they can see themselves as separate, because then they have a greater access to their mind, and beyond. Buddhists have to learn to separate, to override their body to see into their mind. They spend years trying to divorce themselves from their rational mind, to gain clarity and insight into the true meaning of things.

Autists do this naturally! The only trouble is that they don't yet have good control over their nervous system. People such as highly trained Buddhist nuns and monks can get very good at both; it is part of our human capacity.

We are evolving. The reason why so many children are now being diagnosed with autism could be that the vagus nerve is unwell, or irritated by vaccines, environmental toxins or excessive white noise. It could be due to caesareans, birth trauma, post- or pre-birth trauma that can send the baby into a fear response – and it could be that we are evolving.

Aside from all the potential threats we live with, our children are also growing up in a totally new age of technology. Perhaps our autists are, before our eyes, adding a new sequence into the software of the human brain? And perhaps, as it is changing, it is a bit itchy and not so easily integrated with the old system?

Maybe this software is taking a bit of getting used to and we have not yet worked out how to add it in automatically? Perhaps autism is the result of our evolving 'new' system, perhaps our social engagement system is changing and becoming more sophisticated? Perhaps autists are people who are living with a slightly more developed brain – and we just need to figure out how better to integrate this new software?

9. Integrating the Nervous System

The nervous system needs to be soothed and integrated and educated, at all levels. The autist has to begin to engage and command the body.

The more an autist can gain cognition about what is happening, the more they can gain awareness; and with awareness comes control. Essentially, we want autists to come back into their body: to learn to steward it, rather than have the system run *ad hoc*. We want to make them aware, to teach them to engage with their body and have more control. As they begin to learn control, they can begin to learn to steward their body at a very simple, practical level.

What we want to do is to get the nervous system out of the learnt pattern; to physically build up the relationship between the social engagement system and the nervous system; and to build a bigger repertoire of social cues. At every opportunity we want to affirm the autist's ability to tell the body to calm down, and to tell the mind to re-engage and look for something new.

We can teach autists to befriend their body, to understand its learnt patterns and to re-educate it themselves. Living is an embodied experience and reframing autism is a personal journey of discovery and mastery. The autist has to learn to listen to the body. This is a job that is usually done as babies. It is slow and the emphasis is on listening and engaging and re-integrating. It is subtle. It is not achievement-oriented, although once mastered, the achievements can be great.

Autism may not be a neurobiological disorder. It may be a learned response of the autonomic nervous system to trauma or an irritated vagal system. If so, the road ahead lies in re-educating the body, re-informing the body, not just the mind – which takes more than just a 'snap out of it' approach to healing.

You can't simply teach autists social skills, or how to tie their shoelaces, because you/they also have to teach their nervous system. They have to train it to settle and they have to train it to encompass more, to awaken. It is not simply mind over matter, because the body needs to be retrained along with the brain. Ultimately there needs to be a stronger connection between body and brain, and with what we now know about brain plasticity, that is suddenly possible...

10. Brain Plasticity and Autism

> The gift of neuroplasticity (the brain's ability to rewire and create new circuits at any age as a result from input from our environment and our conscious intentions) is that we can create a new level of mind.
>
> *Dr Joe Dispenza, DC*

Lately, we human beings have become very clever. We have figured out that we can change our brains and make them work a whole lot better. We have begun to venture into a whole new paradigm of viewing who we are as humans and what we are capable of.

Neuro (brain) plasticity is an exciting new realm of discovery. We are finding that the brain is open to all sorts of influences and that it can re-wire. We now know that the brain can create new neurons and that it can build all sorts of new neural pathways. What was not working in the brain can now be stimulated, woken up and regenerated. Our brains are like gardens. We can plant new things, water them and bring them to life.

We used to think that our brains were fixed, like a machine, and that we just got what we were born with. Now we know that this is not true. Now we know that our brains are organic; that they are constantly growing and changing. Our brains change with new experiences and we can, if we want to, make all sorts of new neural connections whether we are eight or eighty. We are beginning to learn how easy it can be to make changes. People with strokes, people with chronic learning disabilities, are finding that different brain exercises can make profound changes in their lives.

Science has known since the fifteenth century that the brain can change, but it has not been until recently that we as a community have truly begun to believe in its potential. Individual scientists have been investigating brain plasticity for hundreds of years, but no one in the science community ever took them very seriously so, consequently, neither did we.

It wasn't until the 1960s that things began to change. In 1969, Paul Bach-y-Rita devised a study with a large camera, an electrically stimulated chair and lots of wires and he taught congenitally blind people to recognize a *picture* of the supermodel Twiggy. Essentially he taught them to 'see'. He had worked out how to teach the brain new signals, to teach it to convert tactile (feeling) information into visual information. It worked, and we realized just how much the brain works on signals and physical, electrochemical images.

This study helped us to understand that we are not made like machines, that our brains are actually bundles of electrical impulses and connections, and we shifted into a new paradigm of intelligence; one where we began to believe in the potential of quantum reality, of quantum change.

Paul Bach-y-Rita's study was in response to his father having a debilitating stroke. Because of this, he was inspired to study brain rehabilitation and began to develop therapeutic brain exercises for his father that were so successful at waking up his mind–body connection that his father recovered completely. Bach-y-Rita's father went from being paralysed to mountain climbing! The science community finally began to listen and explore.

In the 1980s, Barbara Arrowsmith began to work with creating brain exercises to improve her brain function. She did this because she grew up with what was then described as a 'mental block', but was actually a range of severe learning disabilities. She read and wrote everything backwards, had trouble conceptualizing language and could not understand the relationships to the point that she found it hard to do things like cross the street. She could not register pain with the left side of her body and was continually getting badly hurt.

Barbara Arrowsmith's life was more than difficult until she came across some research that showed that her problem was related to a particular part of her brain. She decided that she would fix it. She made up exercises to stimulate and wake up the parts of her brain that didn't work so well. It was courageous...and it worked.

Arrowsmith devised all sorts of 'brain' exercises to stimulate her brain. She would do things like draw clocks over and over again; making the times different until her brain began to register the relationship between the hands on the clock.

In a matter of weeks she began to see a massive improvement in how her brain worked. In a matter of months, where originally she could not read and conceptualize, she was able to immerse herself in all sorts of interesting philosophical texts. She could understand in a way she hadn't been able to before. Her brain could finally make sense of things and her life changed for the better.

The brain can change. It was designed to change, to re-organize and improve; it is what it was born to do.

Now that we understand the principles of quantum physics and are beginning to apply these concepts to healing ourselves, we are finding just how remarkable those changes can be.

Our brains have over 300 billion neurons in them and an almost infinite number of possible connections. There are more neurons in our brains than there are stars in the sky. We have so much potential for change and growth, andwe have so much potential for change and growth within autism.

> This is a revolution. We can drive the brain correctively in almost any condition you can think of, ADHD, OCD, Autism…brain plasticity will become the major player of the future.
>
> *Dr Michael Merzenich, world-renowned neuroscientist*

The latest thing in neuroplasticity is 'meta-plasticity'. As meta-cognition is higher awareness of your thinking (meta means 'above', cognition relates to thinking), meta-plasticity is awareness of your brain's plasticity. It sounds very grand, but what it simply means is that people are looking at how to make the brain more able to be plastic, more able to change. They are looking at brain fitness and what is clear is that the more the brain changes, the more it knows how to change. It gets better and better at changing the more changing it does. *Every* brain can improve and change. *Every* brain can get better and better at change.

Within autism there is the possibility of dynamic change. Anat Baniel (author of *Kids Beyond Limits*) and others are doing remarkable work with autists by helping them to reconnect their brain and their body. Being gently helped to learn mastery over their body–mind connection they learn to feel safe, secure and awake; they learn to let the world in. Brain plasticity has a lot to offer the autist.

The only thing to remember is that brain plasticity has to *include the body*. Children learn kinaesthetically. We all learn kinaesthetically. You learn with your body, you process information with your body. Learning is tactile, and sensate. Taking in new information is a physical, biochemical process – it changes you, becomes a part of you.

We have the opportunity to retrain our brain, but it is vital to remember that we do this much more efficiently when we remember to include the body, because *all learning takes place in the body*.

11. The Process of Discovery and Self-Image

Neurophysiological research shows that all physical activity is organized in the brain by images of the person moving through space.

Anat Baniel

All of this information is interpreted in the context of an internal model of the geometry of the body. The body schema appears to be a device for cross-referencing between sensory modalities, and for guiding through space.

Michael Graziano and Matthew Botvinick

Babies make random movements. They don't know that the arms and legs are theirs, but they begin to move and gradually it begins to dawn on them that the sensations they are having are their own. They begin to associate their toes, their feet, arms and legs as their own and they begin to represent them in the mind. They begin to visualize movement, to visualize the body; to see the body moving in the mind.

Neurologically, as a baby moves, the movement leaves a trace of information behind in the brain, and the brain registers these movements as neural patterns, neural circuitry. The brain develops patterns of these movements and registers the body parts that belong to them. It begins to form a three-dimensional representation, a picture of the body, in the mind.

As this happens, the baby has more and more control over their body; they know their body is theirs and they can do more and more. They slowly learn that they can take action. They can tell this arm to move, this leg to kick, and this relationship becomes stronger and stronger. As they want to move, they refer to this 3D image of themself to organize the next pattern of movement.

Movement gradually transfers information to the brain and into thought processes. The baby begins both to experience themself in the world and to realize themself as physical form. Information flows between the baby's growing mind and their growing body. This process of discovery begins very quietly *in utero* and becomes the baby's major occupation for the first few years of life.

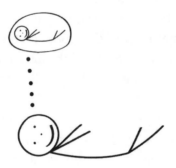

We organize reality in our minds before
we do anything in the physical world

The baby needs to 'relate' to their body so that they can tell it what to do. They need to wire it up; they need to belong to their feet and toes, and they to them. They need to synchronize the mind and the body. This is the job of the baby, and it becomes increasingly complex. They begin with the feet and the toes, and gradually engages with integrating the social system.

As adults, unless we have had a problem, we don't think about moving, we just do it; but babies have to learn this first. Babies are not born knowing how to operate their body. When you are learning to drive, at first you have to be very conscious of everything that you are doing and you start off slowly.

The more you incorporate all the different aspects of the car – the steering, the brakes, the accelerator, the clutch, the road – the more you can drive automatically, without thinking too much. Soon you are out on the highway, among lots of other cars, and your brain can take in the speed, the sounds, the colours, other cars, navigating…and you are set. But first, you have to go really slowly.

Babies, too, have to start off really slowly. They have to become proficient at mastering their body as well as gently setting about the complex task of integrating the sights, sounds and meanings of the world around them. As the baby learns, the movement and the interaction all become natural ways of being – and they all become images in the mind.

But what happens if the baby's attention is diverted by a vagal system that is not working well, or working in overdrive? What if the baby, instead of learning to orchestrate the flow of information, is busy with the itchy jumper from Granny?

Then, instead of focusing solely on building neural images of itself and its world, the baby's awareness is on its inner self. The baby is less attuned to the outside world and to the process of integrating the social engagement system. This is possibly what happens with autism. The child, distracted by discomfort or switched to Immobilize, may not develop a strong image of self to refer to when interacting with the world.

Now, what happens if you don't have a good representation of yourself in your mind? If you can't see your body in 3D in your mind, how do you 'see' it before you move? How do you 'see' it walking down the street? How do you 'see' it talking in a room full of people? You don't consciously do all of these things, they mostly happen automatically, but what would happen if you couldn't do it? Life might get rather confusing.

Think about it. If you are going to clean your room, you sort of see it first, don't you? And it makes it easier. If you are going to a party, you 'see' yourself there having a good time. It may not work out exactly how you wanted, but you get to image yourself and it gives you strength and stability to move into the situation. You can prepare yourself to do something; you can visualize yourself doing well. It is a highly complex act if you think about it. What if you couldn't do this? What if you didn't know how? The world might seem a bit complicated; it might be a bit harder to navigate.

It's possible that autists don't have that luxury. Studies seem to suggest that the autist has an inability to represent mental states. Possibly this is because they miss some vital steps in the early developmental process.

Your 3D brain pattern is your self-image. If you – literally – don't have a clear *self-image*, how are you supposed to learn to engage with the world? How are you supposed to take yourself off to a party? How are you supposed to feel strong? What if this platform, that most people take for granted, is not there?

This, together with the Polyvagal Theory, can change the focus of therapy for autists. If the platform, the self-organizing image, is not strong in the autist and if the body is locked in an adrenal response, then using a fix-it model is only going to be of limited use.

So we can teach social skills, we can teach things like eye contact, tying shoelaces and appropriate manners, but – although these things are useful – if the underlying issues are not addressed then not much is being accomplished. We are merely being mechanical.

What we want is to remember quantum physics! We need to remember that the brain is amazing and can – and will – change. It was *designed* to wire up to the body and it will do it at *any* age, given the right conditions. Your brain loves making spatial patterns; it loves using the social engagement system and integrating the body, and is really itching to do it for you, *at any age.*

12. Anat Baniel and Brain Plasticity

We learn through movement, we turn stimulation into information…with awareness.

Anat Baniel

Nature doesn't grow in straight lines. Nothing in nature is perfectly straight. Our rational brain loves straight lines, they are fun to draw and design buildings with, but they are not natural. We have all grown up learning the classical model of learning: 'get it perfect', 'get it straight', 'there's a proper way of doing things, if you want to get it right'. That's the rational brain way of doing it.

Learning brain plasticity is not a bit like this. It is the opposite of rational: it is natural, organic. We grow like trees, not buildings. We don't erect scaffolding and concrete in our brains, we grow wonderful images; we make music.

If you want to engage with your brain, you need to be open, be mindful that it is a garden not a building, and that there is never just one way of doing things. There are infinite ways of doing things. The point is to engage the brain, to play with its magnificence, and then trust it to do its stuff. It knows what to do – it just needs the right conditions.

Anat Baniel works with a range of childhood conditions, from cerebral palsy to autism. She has a unique way of working with children with special needs that facilitates transformation in a way that ordinary therapies do not. She uses movement with attention and eight other essentials to communicate with the brain to enhance change and learning. As Dr Michael Merzenich wrote in his foreword to Anat's book, *Kids Beyond Limits*:

> Scientists have defined the 'rules' governing brain plasticity. Anat Baniel, working in parallel along a completely different path, has defined almost exactly the same rules. She interprets them in practical and understandable human terms as the 'Nine Essentials', which richly contribute to clinical intervention.

Anat Baniel and her ABM (Anat Baniel Method) have had great success working with autists of all ages. Children under the age of three or four can often lose their diagnosis. She says this is due to a combination of the capacity of the brain to change, and the child having less time to form habits and 'learn' their experience of being on the spectrum.

Anat Baniel calls autism a neuromovement disorder. One of the things she teaches is to do what babies do: lie on the floor, bringing the feet up to the head, bringing the knees up to the head, watching with infinite attention and care the movement of the body. It is about letting the brain and the body reconnect. It is about letting the physical connections come into awareness and attending to the inner sensations. It is learning to follow the feeling of the messages running up and down the body, letting the brain know something new about the body.

As it does this, the brain begins to make new connections, new pathways, and it begins to do what it always wanted to do: it begins to make, or improve, its 3D patterns of the body.

(Although not part of ABM, this exercise also switches on the parasympathetic system. Studies have shown that the parasympathetic system is changed by easing the clenched muscles around the lower spine. Autists, because they spend so much time in a sympathetic state, tend to have very tight muscles here. This exercise relaxes these muscles and permits the flow of information. It also seems to help to reconnect the social engagement system, and to 'switch on' the facial muscles naturally.)

Anat Baniel says that without attention this is simply exercise. This movement is not exercise, it is attending, following and feeling the inner sensations. You have to go slowly, and between each movement you have to stop and let the brain recalibrate. It is movement with attention. It is transforming stimulation into information.

It might not seem like much, but this can be overwhelming for an autist. You need to go very slowly or it can bring on an influx of stimulation that triggers an 'overwhelm' response. Babies don't go fast, they go into a dream-like 'zone' when they are integrating their body.

Now, we can't necessarily get our children to go dreamily, but we can move towards that kind of motion. It is not an operation in making something; it is an operation of engaging, finding and listening. The brain then begins to connect.

How you do the exercises is what matters. You need to remember that we are working with the nervous system, and a flighty one at that. You have to go slowly, you have to work with *awareness*. It is very easy to overload a person with autism, and although it might not look as if you are doing much, the brain is actually processing a great deal of information.

Ultimately we are learning, not to drive the mind, but to give it space to drive itself. We are providing the opportunity for new connections to be made, for new awareness to be harnessed.

> It is essential that the nervous system finds its own intelligence.
>
> *Anat Baniel*

It is beneficial, if you want to experiment with these types of exercises, to learn them first for yourself with a practitioner. We can all learn greater self-awareness and we can only really teach it when we can embody the experience. If you need to, find a practitioner who can teach you or your child how. Just make sure that they understand the principles of brain plasticity, and the principle of child-centred learning.

> Autism provides an opportunity
> for us all to learn higher awareness.

13. The Nine Essentials

Working with children with special needs is not about making them normal. When you respond to the child and see them as perfect and whole – as they are – only then will you have the opportunity to access change, because you are working with the child, and you are aligning with their innate capacity to grow.

Anat Baniel has nine essential steps that she uses when approaching brain plasticity, and they are very effective. They sometimes go a little against the 'scientific' understanding of brain plasticity, but they actually command a greater awareness of how the brain and the body interact. She works on the basis that the brain is a quantum system and that it delights in doing its job organizing the body, so she finds the best pathway through this with each child she works with.

Her success rate with all sorts of childhood challenges is extraordinary. This is a brief look at her work. For a more comprehensive understanding of the approach see *Kids Beyond Limits* (Baniel 2012).

Now, we all naturally know how to do these things. We do them with hobbies, with things that we love to do. Implicitly we employ these techniques; we just don't necessarily always think to employ them with children with autism.

Here are her nine steps in a nutshell.

1. Movement with attention

> When we bring attention to what we feel as we move, the brain immediately starts building billions of new neurological connections that usher in changes, learning and transformation.
>
> *Anat Baniel*

Autists can be quite random with their attention, so we need to learn to direct their attention to themselves and, in particular, direct their awareness to their body and their feeling self. We are bringing them back into their body. To do this we can pay attention to all sorts of movements. Autists are noticeably unaware of themselves physically, so all sorts of occasions can be a way of awakening and making connections.

Anat Baniel says that bringing awareness to everyday activities, bringing awareness to the body, makes all sorts of new connections that were not there before. By noticing, commenting on and making reference to things as they are done, you are strengthening the communication highways in the brain. You are helping the autist to start making distinctions, perceiving differences and learning to feel. You are helping them to locate in the body.

Get the autist to notice the feeling of the hot water as it is coming out of the tap, or notice the shape their hand makes while it is holding something. Which foot do you put in your trousers first? Can you do it differently? Putting your feet on different surfaces – which ones do you like? Why? Picking up marbles with your toes and putting them in a cup; drawing letters on your arm or your back.

All of these things bring awareness and allow the brain to forge a greater body connection and to develop a more complete internal image. The autist can then begin to comfortably allow the flow of information to take place, in all sorts of occasions, effortlessly.

> Do not be surprised
> if all manner of things change for the better
> when your autist begins to awaken.

2. The learning switch

Attention has to be 'on' for learning to take place. The person has to want to learn, and they have to be in the right space for it – it has to be meaningful for them. Otherwise no matter what you do, they will not truly take it into themselves. The child has to want to learn, they have to be open. An open mind is a plastic one, it is ready for change. We cannot force the brain to make new connections, it has to want to, otherwise it will just make strong connections with 'No!'

In the science of neuroplasticity, they say that you need repetition to learn a new skill. But this doesn't always work. Anat Baniel says that repetition can be like brushing the tongue hard with a toothbrush. It's too much, it puts you off and it actually puts you out of a learning state. She says that repetition, especially with a sensitive person, is death to new learning. Repetition works to groove in what is already there, but to learn something new you have to do something different from what you already know.

Learning is tricky. Unless the skill is already in place, unless the underlying mechanism is in place, repetition can become too harsh and the child can switch off. For example, you can motion a baby's arms and legs to teach them to crawl, but until the brain has worked out how to move the arms and legs just so, the baby cannot really do this efficiently. When the brain has wired itself correctly, crawling becomes effortless. The baby just knows what to do.

Forced learning inhibits the learning brain. It takes some time and some space for the brain to recognize something new. When it does, then it can begin to organize movement. Once this movement is in motion, then repetition can become a part of the process of learning.

> As the brain is able to organize action more effectively and with greater ease, the child experiences comfort, anxiety diminishes and the world begins to make sense. The child is able to initiate effective action without prompting or repetitive drilling.
>
> *Anat Baniel*

Repetition is generally mechanistic, boring and heavy-handed. The brain gets turned off and it does not learn. We are playing with a gentle symphony here, not big drums, horns and symbols. We can work up to the big stuff once the little stuff is nicely integrated. Then the big stuff is easy. Familiarity is the way. With familiarity, almost by osmosis, information gets integrated.

The brain is clever and it is quantum. It works much more quickly than we give it credit for. What we need to do is to get out of the mechanistic thinking about the brain and into a quantum brain state. The brain is a wonderful complex, self-organizing, dynamic system that can figure things out for itself – given the right conditions.

If we want the child to be receptive to new thoughts and experiences, we have to promote this receptivity. One way is to be genuinely inquisitive yourself. If you are, your child is more likely to be too. Another way is to find things that are of interest to the child and incorporate learning that way. It is about them opening to the new and, ultimately, they have to be comfortable taking it into their body, because all learning is through the body. It has to feel good, and for the autist this is paramount. So many things do not feel comfortable for the autist, though, as with meta-plasticity, the autist can get better and better at noticing being uncomfortable and working with it.

Familiarity is the key. When you become familiar with something, you know it implicitly. We know how to become familiar with something; we get next to it, we explore it, we 'feel' it. It is not about taming, or training. It is about engaging the brain's natural ability to learn. When you engage the learning brain, change can be extremely rapid.

If your child is tired or cranky, it may not be the best time to ask them to be in a learning zone, but you can make distinctions about this. Ask them if they want to stop. Ask them if they have had enough. Let them bring attention to their experience and let them have the power to choose. This enables greater and greater levels of awareness, empowerment and learning. In this way all times are learning times. They are learning to make distinctions. You are learning to make distinctions.

Just don't overdo it and try too hard – they can see straight through you! You need to be as honestly inquisitive as you want them to be. The more that you can become genuinely inquisitive, the more they will – they learn by osmosis, by familiarity, by being around you.

Learn to unlearn your tendency to impose order.

3. Subtlety

Be delicate. The brain can perceive the tiniest distinctions and does not need to be hammered. The nervous system needs to be able gently to make sense of stimulation – you don't want to bombard it.

Again, think of your tongue. It can perceive all sorts of distinctions of taste and feel, but if you get a brush to it, there's not a lot going on in your brain except revulsion; it's too much. We need subtlety to discern distinctions. This is especially true for autists, as they are easily overstimulated and will shut down.

If we concentrate on the 'effort', if we make a big deal of it, we are not letting the brain quietly get to work. Your brain actually works much better by being given a small piece of information and then being left alone to integrate it. All manner of thinking and learning is actually done while we are not trying. The brain generally does a whole lot of thinking and sorting while we are off doing something else.

Autists are notoriously smart – they can perceive what you want to achieve quickly and they can master things quickly (if you are subtle enough that you do not affront their sensitivities). Half an eyebrow raise, or half a sentence, sometimes is enough to disclose a lot of information. Let the brain work the rest out, let the brain search for the answer a bit. Let the brain engage – if it is handed on a plate, or stuffed down the throat, the brain will switch off.

Your nervous system is like a bird –
you can't force it to sing,
you have to inspire it.
If you bring the right conditions to a person,
they will transform,
re-invent and heal right before your very eyes.

4. Variation

If we did not perceive differences, we would not be able to think or do anything new. The more we can differentiate, get the brain to 'see' the pattern, the difference, the more the brain is able to integrate it and absorb the learning.

This is a skill that the autist needs to learn. The autist can have difficulty perceiving distinctions. They work with what they know and this means that they have limited choice when assessing or responding to a situation. Getting them to perceive distinctions can allow the brain to make new connections and they can begin to see and perceive other possibilities. We can teach this at a very quiet level – as a skill. This skill can then be transferred to other areas of learning. In brain plasticity this is called 'transference'.

Mix things up so the autist gains the ability to perceive differences. Create conditions where there are ample opportunities to perceive differences. If the brain can keep doing this at a higher and higher level, you will see drastic changes. Just make sure that the approach is subtle and gentle. The brain can perceive the most delicate of distinctions, but they need to be clear. The more you learn how to do this, the better you get. The clearer you are with your own distinctions, the easier it will be for your child.

The child needs to feel and perceive the differences themselves, so getting them to learn this through their body is very useful. Thinking up ways to get them to notice distinctions in feeling the difference between things will drive this new ability. Get them to experience the difference between a soft rug and a piece of paper with their feet; try distinguishing between pulling on the big toe versus the little...what does it feel like?

Discuss in minute detail the subtleties of one vanilla ice cream versus another, or the difference between one lollipop and another. Get heaps of lollipops, notice which colours are different, look at all the variation in the shapes they make. Make it fun noticing the differences; focus on the feelings and information that the brain is getting. If you can create a space for noticing differences, you can create a new space in the mind.

Autists often have very little awareness of the impact of their actions. It may seem counter-intuitive, but if your autist is being physical and yelling, then instead of matching it, cowering, or doing whatever you normally do, try changing the tone of your voice or reducing the emotional force – they may start listening and behaving, just out of curiosity if nothing else.

Their brain, just like anyone else's, loves to notice distinctions. Play with it. If they are shouting, name that, without judgement. Tell them it is really loud and that they are 'doing loud' really well, and then ask them if they can shout louder. Then ask them if they can make it even louder. Then ask them if they can shout at a 'normal' level (less than louder). Just by doing this you are giving them distinctions and making it easy for them to be successful in getting quieter. They then may find it easier to go more softly.

The social engagement system
links the face to the heart,
this is why the autist is so hard to read.
If you are having trouble discerning
what your child is feeling, find ways
to learn to read them.
Ask them to draw it for you, ask them to tell you,
make a chart with different colours
representing different emotions
and get them to tick which one is them.
Make coloured 'emotion' stickers
that they can stick on their shirt.
Make up stuff, get creative.
Get them to help think of things,
get them to turn their awareness to
the distinctions of emotions,
inventively.

5. Imagination

In order to grow we have to have a vision of what is possible. So daydreaming, beginning to see possibilities – however small – opens up channels of communication for the brain. Literally, physically, the brain begins to open up to more.

While we are daydreaming, a wide variety of regions in the brain light up – those associated with impulse control, judgment, language, memory, motor function, problem solving, socialization, spontaneity and the processing of sensory information.

Anat Baniel

Daydreaming allows the brain the freedom and flexibility to 'move around' what it already knows, to go beyond what it has already acquired and invent new possibilities. The brain comes to life with daydreaming; and play, not repetition or instructive learning, is vital for learning, because it opens this space.

The brain doesn't know the difference between reality and a dream – so find ways to help the child gently engage with their dreams! What would you love to do...? What is the most beautiful thing you can imagine...? Imagine if you could... Imagine if we went this way...did it this way... Opening up the possibility for change, however small, begins a new train of thought and encourages new neural pathways.

This is not always easy for the autist, so take it slowly. Keep it simple. Don't jump on it. Curiosity is good. What if...? What do you think would happen if...? Start to talk about the world, the people in it. Start to visualize smiling, interacting gracefully. Listen to self-help 'I can' kind of audios, listen to soothing music. Teach the body to relax and the mind to open.

> Stay off computers for long intervals –
> research is showing that computers and
> computer games bring the body to a state of FFI.
> We go into switched off and high stress,
> whether we perceive it or not.
> You cannot learn well in this state,
> and it is not conducive to the imagination.
> Computers are a fact of modern life,
> we don't need to eradicate them;
> we just need to be aware of their limitations.

6. Go slow

Autists need to go slowly to feel safe. Their system seeks survival and safety. Their system will work against change; it is uneasy with new things. So we need to go slowly. We need to learn that change is good. We need to slowly integrate change, so that it is *safe* to change. We need to make change the habit; we need to encourage the person's ability to change.

Anat Baniel says that when learning goes from being a conscious action to an unconscious one, it turns into integrated action. Your brain is structured to work as a whole. It likes to work fast and it has to work fast to get everything done without conscious awareness – otherwise everything would take too long.

The brain gains speed when it has incorporated its learning. Without going slowly, it is hard to learn. The brain needs to observe the pieces of the puzzle and then let it make sense. A little bit here, a little bit there, a little more skill in the right direction. Then a little more, a little more, and suddenly it all comes together.

When we think fast, we can only do what we already know. Going slowly gets the brain's attention and stimulates the formulation of new neural patterns. It also gets us out of automatic mode in our movements, speech, thought and social interactions and allows awareness of where we are at.

If you slow down, you also get the child to differentiate between how they are doing something and the outcome. They can begin to perceive how they might do it better. Also, we all learn by osmosis, so watch how *you* approach something…and see how *you* can do it differently – and they will follow.

And remember, it is easy to forget that the things that are easy for you are not easy for the autist. For them, the basic building blocks often are not there. What is effortless for you is not effortless for them – yet.

7. Flexible goals

Back off from performance outcomes. You need to trust the process. If you overdo it with autists, if you push, if you yank and control the outcome, you will lose them. Like a bird, if you try to control them, they will fly away. If it is too much, they will switch off and no learning will take place. It has to be easy. New things can't be too hard; all they do then is concentrate on it being hard, then they focus on failure.

Keep the focus open. Autists are very good at knowing what they can't do and are generally very self-negative; they have learnt not to expect much. The goal, as such, is to diminish the hardwired 'I can't', the 'No!', and replace it with 'Yes!'

This is 'neuro-pruning'. It is a good gardening term. You can prune neurons as easily as you can build them. You lessen your view on the negative and focus on what is good. In brain plasticity, the motto is 'what thrives survives'. Make it fun, make it a pleasure – we all grow well with our parasympathetic system in play.

Anat Baniel says, 'We will know when we get there!' It is about playing with ideas; it is not about concrete, rational goals. The goals are to awaken and develop, to plant and grow the brain garden. The play aspect is vital, it has to be fun and it is why you have to be 'just going somewhere', not anywhere in particular. You are making a new garden, a new, stronger system; you cannot have an outcome curriculum for that. The more organic you make it the better. Any sense of failure, any getting it wrong – for carer or for child – just takes you out of the learning space. So when you find yourself here, be especially kind to yourself and take a break. Rome was not built in a day. No pressure.

With brain plasticity, there are things going on under the surface that for a while you can't see. We can think that nothing is happening. It is important here to remember to look at distinctions, perceiving tiny distinctions. Watch the change happening, not the end goal. Tiny seeds are being planted and watered and they can seem to go slowly...until one day you look and you have a totally new person standing in front of you!

> In a quantum system there are no such things as small changes...once there has been a shift, once the brain starts learning, it can learn exponentially.
>
> *Anat Baniel*

8. Enthusiasm

Subtle changes on the outside can make huge changes inside, in the brain's wiring. If we are patient, all of a sudden these imperceptible changes can magically roll together to become real change – so much so that you can almost forget that the child could not do this or that a few months ago. Their new behaviour has become natural to them and to you.

But to start with, you need to take quiet delight in the small changes. The child picks this up and feels reassured and encouraged. Enthusiasm is great! Kids need lots of encouragement and joy, just make it gentle.

We are growing something new, something more intelligent than was there before. When we watch for the green shoots of new growth, they don't necessarily look big, but it is important to notice them and rejoice, because they do signify big things to come.

Make it about the process not the outcome; keep a lot of it to yourself. An autist is a flighty bird, they do not need boisterous affirmation. They are subtle enough that they will read the quietest 'yes'. Take profound, quiet pleasure...

A skill is only the byproduct of higher and higher levels of complexity – start where you start and keep noticing the complexity, not the goal.

Anat Baniel

If you need to, write notes.
Take a baseline of things they can do,
small things, things they can't.
Keep a journal,
it can be astonishing to read back on
and can show you how far you have come.

9. Awareness

Building awareness is our highest function. It is our newest function. When you apply awareness to all your activities you upgrade your brain, because you are encouraging new neural connections. Anat Baniel calls it 'awaring', because it is an activity. Awaring is the opposite of automated and compulsive. It is accessing all the subtleties, distinctions and nuances to allow you to be fully alive and present. We can all, always, increase our awareness.

One of the latest neuroplasticity terms is 'self-directed neuroplasticity', which refers to understanding the physics of the interface between mind/consciousness and brain. Really, all it means is that we are all in charge of our own brain plasticity, our own awareness. No one can do it for us. It is the work for all human beings to become more aware, autists included. Awareness is our natural birthright as evolving human beings.

Belief

Anat Baniel talks about the power of belief in imagination, and I am going to reiterate it here. All new things require belief. They require vision before they can manifest. You have to 'see' it before it can exist. It means that, inside you, there is a small (or large) picture that sees the healing potential in your child.

You have to believe enough, or suspend belief. If you do not think something is going to work, if you are not open, you will not look for distinctions, you will be unsubtle and unenthusiastic.

You cannot do anything without a vision. As a parent, teacher or carer you have to see the possibilities and be open to them... And be open to possibilities that you cannot even imagine!

14. Some Other Integration Techniques

Studies have shown that the Emotional Freedom Technique (EFT) has a direct effect on reducing cortisol levels and calming down Fight or Flight. It provides a balance between the parasympathetic and the sympathetic nervous systems, getting everything to calm down and flow smoothly. It engenders a calm emotional state which promotes health, wellbeing and clarity of mind.

Autism is a physical manifestation, so working with the body as well as the mind gives a clarity of connection that is not possible otherwise. We live an embodied experience and it is this that the autist is yet to learn. Some or all of these techniques may prove useful to you. You can find links to them at the back of the book in the section 'Some Resources to Explore'.

Emotional Freedom Technique

The Emotional Freedom Technique (EFT) involves tapping on acupoints, specific acupressure or meridian points, while talking through emotional issues. The tapping sends signals directly to the stress centres of the mid-brain. It accesses the amygdala (the part of your brain that initiates FFI) and gets it to calm down. Tapping while talking through the issue simultaneously deals with stress on a physical and emotional level. It calms the mind and the body and helps to re-educate both.

This technique helps to calm and reorganize the brain. It is a great thing to do when you are feeling stressed or un-calm. There is a full-body version, but I like this little one as you can do it anywhere, any time, and you don't look too silly.

If you are worried or anxious, you can say something like 'even though I am worried' or 'even though I am scared'... and do this tapping technique.

Tap the outside of your thumbs – the side closest to you – with your middle fingers; and then the outside of all your fingers (near your cuticles) with your thumbs. What you are doing is tapping all of your major meridian points, and soothing the body. Do this for a few minutes whilst talking through your problem. It is very calming. This works very well with children. It works because it engages the brain and the body. The references to EFT at the back of this book are well worth a look.

Structural Integration

Another body strategy is Structural Integration (or Rolfing), designed by Ida Rolf. It very gently wakes the body up to where it should be and better aligns the body in the gravitational field. By resetting the body's learnt patterns, it allows increased use of balance at finer levels of the neuro-fascial-musculo-skeletal system. It promotes physical adaptability, resilience and general wellbeing, as well as reducing biomechanically caused pain.

This strategy gently and very effectively retrains the body. It incorporates moves that release the muscles around the lower spine, as well as around the jaw and face. It is very good for teens and adults, as they have become much more entrenched in their body learning than younger children, although young autists can get a good deal of benefit from it.

> Rolfing Structural Integration has the ability to dramatically alter a person's posture and structure. Rolfing SI can potentially resolve discomfort, release tension and alleviate pain. Rolfing SI aims to restore flexibility, revitalize your energy and leave you feeling more comfortable in your body. The genius of the work rests on Dr Rolf's insight that the body is more at ease and functions most effectively when its structure is balanced in gravity.
>
> *The Rolf Institute of Structural Integration*

The Listening Project Protocol

Dr Porges has found that he can improve autism by stimulating the social engagement system. With the use of acoustic sessions using the frequencies of the human voice he has shown that he can stimulate the social engagement system and get it working more efficiently.

He initiated The Listening Project Protocol, when he was director of the Brain–Body Center at the University of Illinois in Chicago, where he worked with autists to exercise and enhance the social engagement system. He uses *voice frequencies* to soothe and promote positive emotional states that are associated with safety. He employs computer altered vocal music, rather than other sounds, since the voice stimulates and exercises the neural (brain) regulation of the middle ear muscles and other aspects of the social engagement system. The body processes the sound of the voice differently from other acoustic signals. It is the most soothing.

Integrated Listening Systems

This is another tool that is used by families of autists. Many find that it provides positive changes in the ability of their child to participate in the world.

> Integrated Listening programs effectively 're-train' parts of the brain involved in learning, communicating and moving. Combining an auditory program with specific visual and balance activities allows iLs to rapidly strengthen neurological pathways and improves the ability to learn and to process information.
>
> The three main systems for organizing sensory input – visual, auditory and balance (vestibular) – are highly interrelated. Exercising all three simultaneously is a holistic approach which can help build comprehension in the classroom and build literacy, numeracy and communication skills. This holistic approach also helps clients of any age to feel sharper, more focused, and more self-confident.
>
> *iLs Australia*

Anat Baniel Method

This method evolved from Anat Baniel's professional work as a clinical psychologist and dancer. Close collaboration with Moshe Feldenkrais and the experience born of 30 years of remarkable outcomes with thousands of children and adults brought about a unique method that she has been able to reproduce and teach to others. Through innovative movement exercises and the 'Nine Essentials', new neural patterns are created which give increased strength, flexibility, vitality and awareness to the individual.

ABM is a cutting-edge, science-based approach that utilizes practical brain plasticity techniques which dramatically enhance physical, cognitive, emotional and creative performance.

Anat Baniel defines her work as a NeuroMovement® approach. She does special mastery training to teach her practitioners how to work with children with special needs and specifically with children on the spectrum. With more and more research emerging as to the movement components of autism spectrum disorders, Anat Baniel's approach seems destined to become an integral part of any successful strategy for working with children on the spectrum. References to her website and to fascinating YouTube videos are at the back of this book.

Feldenkrais Method

The Feldenkrais Method works to bring about an improved interplay with the body via the central nervous system. It works to improve physical function and promotes general wellbeing by increasing students' awareness of themselves and by expanding their repertoire of movement. Feldenkrais taught that increasing a person's kinaesthetic and proprioceptive self-awareness of functional movement could reduce pain and improve motion.

Classes are called 'Awareness Through Movement'. A Feldenkrais practitioner guides the participants through a gentle sequence of movement explorations and, as they move, attention is drawn to the movement. Participants learn to observe their movements, and learn easier ways of moving in everyday activities.

Individual lessons are called 'Functional Integration'. This is a hands-on process. The practitioner guides movements through precise touch while the client lies or sits, comfortably clothed, on a low padded table. The practitioner brings present movement habits into focus and shares new movement options. The learning is then applied to daily activities such as standing, walking and sitting.

A major difference between this and ABM is that many Feldenkrais practitioners do not have the experience of working with children and they do not train specifically with brain plasticity and the need to be organic in their approach. Autists need a particularly individual programme, tailored around them and open to change. Look for a Feldenkrais practitioner who has experience in this area.

Body/Mind training

Physical exercises are excellent for retraining the mind–body connection. Juggling, dancing, martial arts, swimming and gentle horse-riding all help the autist to calmly re-engage with the body and retrain the brain to process visual and auditory information. Horses seem to be particularly soothing at a body level, but a quietly-spoken martial artist may be equally beneficial.

Bothmer

Bothmer was developed in 1921 by Fritz von Bothmer after being invited by Rudolf Steiner to develop a gymnastics programme for his school.

Bothmer is holistic movement training. It teaches the child to take hold of their body in stages, to integrate the mind–body connection, physically, emotionally and consciously. It encourages the child to take hold of their body with joy and imagination. Bothmer is 'a play between weight and lightness', between gravity and levity, and it prepares a space for creative activity. Bothmer is still taught in Steiner Schools today.

15. Where We Go From Here

Success is a paradox. It is keeping open to possibility, whilst braving the wind, whilst keeping your eye on the prize.

You can explore all sorts of forms of therapy, and it is good to explore. No one thing will work for everybody. Keeping open to new experiences is what keeps us alive and aware. Most of all, I encourage you to really embrace the ideas in this book. Neuroplasticity is a playground for us all; it is not simply for the professionals. We can all learn to play and engage with our learning brain, and like any good garden, we can all keep growing.

Autism has been seen as 'incurable'. What does this really mean? It is incurable because we have not yet found a way to understand it, to make it an 'illness' that can be cured. Maybe this is because it isn't one in the classical sense? Maybe it is a cluster of learnt body/brain responses that disallow a certain way of being and maybe we can retrain that? There is so much more for us to understand.

In his book *How the Mind Works*, Steven Pinker says: 'The linguist Noam Chomsky once suggested that our ignorance can be divided into problems and mysteries. When we face a problem, we may not know its solution, but we have insight, increasing knowledge and an inkling of what we are looking for. When we face a mystery, however, we can only stare in wonder and bewilderment, not knowing what an explanation would even look like.'

We have been looking at autism with wonder and bewilderment. Now, with the Polyvagal Theory, we have the ability to upgrade our understanding of autism to a problem that we can begin to play with. Now we have an inkling of where to look.

The Polyvagal Theory provides a framework for autism that allows all the other theories to rest on. It provides an umbrella under which all the other ideas about the cause of autism – nutrients, antigens, genetics, metabolism – can sit quite neatly. All of these things make sense within this theory. All of these things can affect the vagal nerve and disturb the natural integration of the social engagement system.

The Polyvagal Theory illuminates why there are so many varied autistic traits. Some autists can't speak, some are greatly affected by noise, others by fluorescent lights; some are fixated on objects or activities; some have highly intolerant digestion, temper tantrums and so on.

It makes sense that each autist is affected differently by their unique physical and emotional circumstances; their particular sensory system. We human beings are unique and varied and we all have to make sense of our personal world. Each and every autist is embodying a personal response to a personal experience. Like anyone, each has their own particular genetic make-up, their own particular nervous system, and their diverse social, emotional and physical environments to grow up in. Within this paradigm it makes sense that there is so much diversity.

The human system is designed to adapt, and this is what autists are doing. From a very early age they are adapting to a set of difficult physical and/or emotional symptoms that secondarily affect their ability to communicate and be in the world.

I encourage you to embrace the notion that the vagal system plays a major role in the onset of autism and to embrace the notion that we all have the propensity for autism – that it is part of a natural human response to trauma and fear. The more you can see that it is a normal shutdown response that has been left on too long, the more you can feel what it feels like.

The more you can empathize with the autist and be on the same page, the more you will see change. Whatever we look at changes; and whatever we look at with love, affection and recognition flowers under our gaze. Autists are the same as everyone else. They feel the same as everyone else, they want the same things, and they are always hoping to be seen for who they really are. Simply being seen opens their hearts and gives them hope. Hope gives way to faith, faith to belief, and with belief you can achieve anything.

Conclusion

Every now and again we come across something that takes our breath away, both by its simplicity and by the fact that somewhere buried deep in us, we have always known it to be true.

I still remember my first day at Kindergarten. My twin sister took one look at the playground full of children and ran to them with a whoop of delight. I just stood there thinking, 'What am I supposed to do with that?' Interacting with strangers, large (or small) groups of people, did not come naturally. While the other kids were off playing, I was painting white elephants on white paper. As I got older I got better at hiding it, and playing to my strengths. I was also smart and pretty, so people would often think me cold, aloof (or boring), rather than suspect that I was shut down with an unnamed fear. I was more than shy.

While I have never been diagnosed with autism, I have certainly had some of the struggles and insights that people 'on the spectrum' invariably get to know and so the subject fascinates me both personally and professionally.

The work of Stephen Porges delighted me when I read it; it was as if the sun had come out – suddenly all sorts of things made sense. Porges' theory has bridged the gap between the mind and the body. Stephen Porges has made scientifically explainable what we understand intuitively about ourselves. He has made a huge contribution to our understanding of not only autists, but how we all interact with our world, and just how much our bodies are involved in our psychology.

This idea of body psychology has been implicit in all the personal work that I have done to gain better control over my mind–body connection. It has always been very natural to me to see this shut down as a body issue because, when it happens, *you know that your body is shutting down.*

Professionally, since my university days, I have been riveted by this subject. It has been the focus of all my work and thinking. I have researched a lot over the years, but Dr Porges' work has brought it all to a new playing field for me. The more I talked about this theory to autist friends, the more it was clear that it resonated for them too, and they all said, 'That just makes so much sense!'

Once I had read Dr Porges' work I had to write this book. It is important that psychology is available to the lay person. It matters that we can be empowered to make changes in our lives. It is important, too, that we keep an open mind and constantly challenge the prevailing ideology. Science is always changing, and so it never knows everything; and with autism, we do not seem to know very much at all.

The work of Dr Stephen Porges can change what we know about autism and can allow a significant shift in our understanding, yet not many people are aware of it – many professionals included.

The work of Anat Baniel is inspiring and I suggest you look at her work via YouTube. She is not working miracles, but you could be forgiven for thinking so. What she is doing is applying the best of neuroplasticity, with an extensive understanding of the body, to manifest wondrous healing for people. She is also extending this knowledge worldwide, showing us just how easy it is, how it is possible.

It is easy. When I discovered her 'Nine Essentials', I realized I already knew them intrinsically. I have always approached myself, my children and my clients in this manner; it is natural for me. What was wonderful was to hear it said with such clarity and strength. Anat Baniel's ability to articulate the subtleties of human learning, with special needs in particular, is both remarkable and wonderful. Her Nine Essentials allow us to conceptualize working at this subtle level, and I do recommend you peruse her book for a deeper level of understanding.

This book provides a beautiful and wide consideration of autism. While the Polyvagal Theory looks more at the *why*, the Anat Baniel Method is more focused on the *how*. Apart they are fascinating, but lovingly pieced together with the basis of neuroplasticity, they make an extraordinary picture for us.

These theories allow us to envision a whole new way of approaching and understanding autism. I hope that in the future autism is, for us all, a little easier to fathom, a little easier to play with, a little easier to embrace.

Some Resources to Explore

Baniel, A. (2012) *Kids Beyond Limits*. New York: Perigee (an imprint of Penguin).

Blomberg, H. and Dempsey, M. (2011) *Movements That Heal, Rhythmic Movement Training and Primitive Reflex Integration*. Sunnybank Hills, QLD, Australia: BookPal.

Feldenkrais, M. (1990) *Awareness Through Movement: Easy-to-Do Health Exercises to Improve Your Posture, Vision, Imagination, and Personal Awareness*. San Francisco, CA: HarperCollins.

Hannaford, C. (2005) *Smart Moves: Why Learning Is Not All In Your Head*. Salt Lake City, UT: Great River Books.

Herbert, M. and Weintraub, K. (2012) *The Autism Revolution: Whole-Body Strategies for Making Life All It Can Be*. New York: Ballantine Books.

Mitchell, C. (2012) *A New Sensory Self-Awareness: Tools to Experience the Body-To-Brain Connection: Part I*. Kamuela, HI: Wellness Through Movement. Available at http://wellnessthroughmovement.com.

Emotional Freedom Technique

www.dummies.com/how-to/content/the-hand-tapping-points-in-emotional-freedom-techn.html

www.thetappingsolution.com

Tapping World Summit – How to Tap

www.youtube.com/watch?v=0sLaPUppAxo

Structural Integration

www.rolf.org/about

Rolf Structural Integration Demo Part 4

www.youtube.com/watch?v=ycqBQVX32oI

www.rolfguild.org/about/structural-integration

The Listening Project Protocol

Porges, S.W., Bazhenova, O.V., Bal, E., Carlson, N., Sorokin, Y., Heilman, K.J., Cook, K.H. and Lewis, G.F. (2014) 'Reducing Auditory Hypersensitivities in Autistic Spectrum Disorder: Preliminary Findings Evaluating the Listening Project Protocol.' *Frontiers in Pediatrics.* Doi:10.3389/fped.2014.00080http://dx.doi.org/10.3389/fped.2014.0080.

http://stephenporges.com

Integrated Listening Systems

www.listen4life.com

www.integratedlistening.com.au

Anat Baniel Method

Treatment for Autism in Children – The Anat Baniel Method and Treatment of Autism in Children

www.anatbanielmethod.com

www.youtube.com/watch?v=7-9NrVePsTA

Anat Baniel – Method for Children

www.youtube.com/watch?v=-QRYJyRiYDE

Stephen Porges

http://stephenporges.com

Feldenkrais Method

www.feldenkrais.org.au/about-feldenkrais-method

What is the Feldenkrais method*

    www.youtube.com/watch?v=e_i5QuIqcQo

Body/Mind training

Horse Therapy Helps Autistic Boy

    www.youtube.com/watch?v=ICqDiCBxPDQ

Bothmer

Bothmer Movement International

    www.youtube.com/watch?v=Nxgpi-niYzg

Bothmer Israel – Stickwork lesson

    www.youtube.com/watch?v=vxmdN81O5r4

SI 2013 Rhythm 02

    www.youtube.com/watch?v=yswzgDVPSCo

Bibliography

American Psychiatric Association (2013) *Diagnostic and Statistical Manual of Mental Disorders, DSM-5.* Arlington, VA: APA. Available at http://dsm.psychiatryonline.org.

Arrowsmith-Young, B. (2012) *The Woman Who Changed Her Brain: How I Left My Learning Disabilities Behind and Other Stories of Cognitive Transformation.* New York: Simon and Shuster.

Arrowsmith-Young, B. (2013, August) *How We Can Shape Our Minds.* Octagon Theatre, University of Western Australia, Perth, Australia.

Bach-y-Rita, P. (1967) 'Sensory Plasticity.' *Acta Neurologica Scandinavica* 43: 417 – 426.

Baniel, A. (Producer) (2007) *ABM for Children with Special Needs 2 Day Workshop* (DVD program). USA.

Baniel, A. (2012) *Kids Beyond Limits.* New York: Perigee (an imprint of Penguin).

Bonini, L., Ferrari, P.F. and Fogassi, L. (2013) 'Neurophysiological bases underlying the organization of intentional actions and the understanding of others' intention.' *Consciousness and Cognition* 22, 3, 1095–1104.

Bruer, J. (1999) *The Myth of The First Three Years: A New Understanding Of Early Brain Development And Lifelong Learning.* New York: The Free Press.

Chong, T.T-J., Cunnington, R., Williams, M.A., Kanwisher, N. and Mattingley, J.B. (2008) 'fMRI Adaption reveals mirror neurons in human inferior parietal cortex.' *Current Biology 18*, 20, 1576–1580. doi:10.1016/j.cub.2008.08.068.

Collins, P. (2004) *Not Even Wrong: Adventures in Autism.* New York: Bloomsbury.

Cottingham, J.T., Porges, S.W. and Richmond, K. (1988) 'Shifts in pelvic inclination angle and parasympathetic tone produced by Rolfing soft tissue manipulation.' *Physical Therapy 68*, 9, 1364–1370.

Cottingham, J.T., Porges, S.W. and Lyon, T. (1988) 'Effects of soft tissue mobilization (Rolfing Pelvic Lift) on parasympathetic tone in two age groups.' *Physical Therapy 68*, 3, 352.

Dispenza, J. (2013) *Breaking the Habit of Being Yourself: How to Lose Your Mind and Create a New One.* Carlsbad, CA: Hay House, Inc.

Doidge, N. (2012) Foreword. In B. Arrowsmith-Young *The Woman Who Changed Her Brain: How I Left My Learning Disability Behind and Other Stories of Cognitive Transformation.* New York: The Free Press.

Feldenkrais, M. (1981) *The Elusive Obvious.* Capitola, CA: Meta Publications.

Glezerman, T.B. (1981) *Autism and the Brain: Neurophenomenological Interpretation.* New York: Springer.

Graziano, M.S.A. and Botvinick, M.M. (2002) 'How the Brain Represents the Body: Insights from Neurophysiology and Psychology.' In W. Prinz and B. Hommel (eds) *Common Mechanisms in Perception and Action.* New York: Oxford University Press.

McPartland, J. and Klin, A. (2006) 'Asperger's syndrome.' *Adolescent Medical Clinics 17* (3) 771–88. doi:10.1016/j.admecli.2006.06.010. PMID 17030291.

Pinker, S. (1997) *How the Mind Works.* New York: Norton.

Porges, S.W. (2005) 'The Vagus: A Mediator of Behavioral and Visceral Features Associated With Autism.' In M.L. Bauman and T.L. Kemper (eds) *The Neurobiology Of Autism* (2nd edition). Baltimore, MD: The John Hopkins University Press.

Porges, S.W. (2011) *The Polyvagal Theory: Neurophysiological Foundations of Emotions, Attachment, Communication, and Self-regulation.* New York: Norton.

Rochat, P. (1998) 'Self-perception and action in infancy.' *Experimental Brain Research 123*, 1–2, 102–109. doi:10.1007/s002210050550.

Roll, J.P.R. and Velay, J.L. (1991) 'Proprioception as a link between body space and extra-personal space.' *Cognition 21*, 37–46.

About the Author

Holly Bridges has a degree in psychology and runs a therapeutic consultancy, License To Think, teaching people how to apply and cultivate brain plasticity. She also works for a leading autism service provider, working with young adults. Holly has worked as an autism carer, coordinator and community inclusion project officer and has been nominated in the 'Excellence in Personal and Community Support' category of the 2015 Disability Support Awards Australia – National Disability Services for her work in autism support. Holly lives in Perth, Western Australia.

Find out more about her upcoming workshops and books:

http://licensetothink.com.au

www.facebook.com/LicensetoThink

Index